Incredible Fish

John Townsend

www.raintreepublishers.co.uk
Visit our website to find out more information about **Raintree** books.

To order:
☎ Phone 44 (0) 1865 888113
📄 Send a fax to 44 (0) 1865 314091
💻 Visit the Raintree Bookshop at www.raintreepublishers.co.uk to browse our catalogue and order online.

First published in Great Britain by Raintree, Halley Court, Jordan Hill, Oxford OX2 8EJ, part of Harcourt Education. Raintree is a registered trademark of Harcourt Education Ltd.

Editorial: Charlotte Guillain and Diyan Leake
Design: Michelle Lisseter and Kamae Design
Picture Research: Maria Joannou
Production: Jonathan Smith

Originated by Ambassador Litho Ltd
Printed and bound in Hong Kong, China by South China Printing Company

ISBN 1 844 43330 7
08 07 06 05 04
10 9 8 7 6 5 4 3 2 1

British Library Cataloguing in Publication Data
Townsend, John
Incredible Fish. – (Incredible Creatures)
597
A full catalogue record for this book is available from the British Library.

Acknowledgements
The publisher would like to thank the following for permission to reproduce photographs: Ardea p. 30; Corbis pp. 6 top (Robert Yin), 17 (Tim Wright), 48 (Jeffrey L. Rotman); FLPA pp. 4–5, 9 left, 10–11, 11, 12–13, 13, 14, 16–17, 19 bottom, 19 top, 20, 22–3, 24, 25, 26 top, 34, 35, 36, 43, 45 top, 48–9, 50, 50–1, 52; Image Quest 3–D p. 41; NASA p. 46 (Jacques Descloitres, MODIS Rapid Response Team, GSFC); Nature Photo Library pp. 28 top (John Downer), 31; NHPA pp. 4, 5 top, 5 middle, 5 bottom, 6 bottom, 7, 8, 9 right, 10, 12, 15 bottom, 15 top, 16, 20–1, 22, 26 bottom, 27, 28 bottom, 29, 30–1, 33, 34–5, 37 top, 37 bottom, 38 left, 38–9, 39 right, 40, 40–1 (Bill Wood), 42–3, 42, 45 bottom, 44, 46–7, 47, 49; Oxford Scientific Films pp. 18, 24–5, 32–3, 32 left; Photofusion p. 51; Science Photo Library p. 23 (Alexis Rosenfeld); www.jjphoto.dk p. 21

Cover photograph of a piranha reproduced with permission of Getty Images (National Geographic/Paul A. Zahl)

The publishers would like to thank Jon Pearce for his assistance in the preparation of this book.

Every effort has been made to contact copyright holders of any material reproduced in this book. Any omissions will be rectified in subsequent printings if notice is given to the publishers.

Disclaimer
All the Internet addresses (URLs) given in this book were valid at the time of going to press. However, due to the dynamic nature of the Internet, some addresses may have changed, or sites may have changed or ceased to exist since publication. While the author and publishers regret any inconvenience this may cause readers, no responsibility for any such changes can be accepted by either the author or the Publishers.

The paper used to print this book comes from sustainable resources.

Contents

Fantastic fish!   4

Meet the family   6

Amazing bodies   12

Feeding   18

Breeding   28

Defence   34

Weird and wonderful   40

Fish in danger   46

Find out more   52

Glossary   54

Index   56

Any words appearing in the text in bold, **like this**, are explained in the Glossary. You can also look out for them in the 'Wild words' bank at the bottom of each page.

Fantastic fish!

Fast and old

- Tuna fish, swordfish and some sharks are among the fastest fish. Some can reach 80 kilometres (50 miles) per hour in short bursts.

- Sturgeon fish can live for over 50 years but we still do not know if other fish can live longer.

What is a fish? This may seem a simple question but the answer is not quite so easy. Do all fish live in water, have shiny scales and fins? Some do, some do not.

There are three main types of fish and they live in either fresh water or salty sea water all round the world. Only a very few **species** can live in both sorts of water.

The three types of fish are:

1 Bony fish. This is the biggest group, with about 20,000 species. That is 95 per cent of all fish.
2 Bendy fish. There are about 900 species of these – with softer skeletons that are **cartilaginous**.
3 Jawless fish. These are **parasites** with mouths that suck on other fish.

▲ **Shoals** of tuna fish dart through the sea at great speed.

Wild words   cartilaginous   having soft bendy gristle rather than bone
parasite   animal or plant that lives in or on another living thing

Bony fish

Fish were the first **vertebrates** to exist on Earth. Bony fish have skeletons made of bone and they come in many shapes and sizes. They usually have their mouth at the very front of their head. These fish are found in freshwater rivers and lakes or in salty oceans. Very few fish can move from one type of water to the other, as the two **environments** are very different.

Bendy fish

Bendy fish have a much softer skeleton. It is made of cartilage, the same soft material that makes the shape of your nose. Many of these fish, including rays and sharks, have their mouths on their underside. Nearly all of these fish live in the sea.

Jawless fish

Jawless fish, such as hagfish, make the third group. They do not have proper fins and tails. Lampreys are jawless fish that live in the sea and in fresh water.

Find out later...

What was the great fish discovery of the 20th century?

What was the monster of Crofton Pond?

What is the most shocking fish?

▲ The great white shark can open its jaws to a metre wide!

species   type of living animal or plant
vertebrate   any animal that has a skeleton with a backbone

Meet the family

Did you know...?

- If you keep a goldfish in a dark room, it will slowly turn white.

- The dwarf goby is the smallest fish at 1 centimetre long.

All fish are different, but many are similar in some ways. So what do most fish have in common?

Fishy features

- Many fish have fins to **propel** them forward and for steering.
- Fish are usually smooth and **streamlined** (torpedo-shaped) to help them slip through the water. Fish are slippery, which helps them to move smoothly through the water without **friction**.
- Nearly all fish have slimy scales to keep their body waterproof. Scales come in different types and shapes but they are like little plates of armour that overlap to protect the fish.
- Fish have tiny **sensors** along their head and sides. These sensors detect pressure changes in the water when other animals come near.

▲ Goby fish come in many sizes and colours.

▲ The sea bass is a typical streamlined shape and covered in scales.

Wild words   camouflage   colour that matches the background
friction   drag or force when things rub together

- Fish come in all colours and patterns. Some have very good **camouflage** and some can change their colour or pattern to match different surroundings. Fish that swim at the surface often have white bellies, silvery sides and dark blue backs. This makes it difficult for **prey** and **predators** to spot them. When seen from above, the darker shade blends in with the sea, and when seen from below, the pale colour blends with the light from the sky.
- All fish are 'cold blooded'. This means their body temperature is about the same as the water around them. Unlike **mammals**, such as humans, they do not make their own body heat. Like **reptiles** and **amphibians**, they depend on their **environment** to keep them at the right temperature.

▼ A diver is safe near the mouth of the whale shark.

Big fish

The largest fish is the whale shark, which is almost 1500 times bigger than the goby. Some whale sharks are the size of a bus and reach 14 metres in length. They can weigh up to 12 tonnes. The next biggest fish is the basking shark, at around 12 metres long. These fish do not attack humans.

predator   animal that hunts and eats other animals
streamlined   torpedo-shaped

Protected

A coelacanth can be the same size and weight as a human. Very little is known about this very rare fish, which is now protected by law. It lives in undersea caves 200–700 metres deep and it seems to be active only at night.

Bony and baffling

Fossils of bony skeletons show that an **ancient** type of fish was around long before the dinosaurs. Scientists thought this fish had been **extinct** for millions of years. Then came the find of the 20th century. In 1938 the fish appeared alive and well in the Indian Ocean near Africa. It is called a coelacanth ('see-la-kanth'). Scientists think this **species** has remained unchanged for 400 million years, even though each fish only lives for up to 60 years.

Others have been found since. A scientist from California was on holiday in Indonesia in 1997. In the middle of a fish market he saw a strange blue fish on one of the slabs. His mouth dropped open as he realized it was a coelacanth. Another one had been found.

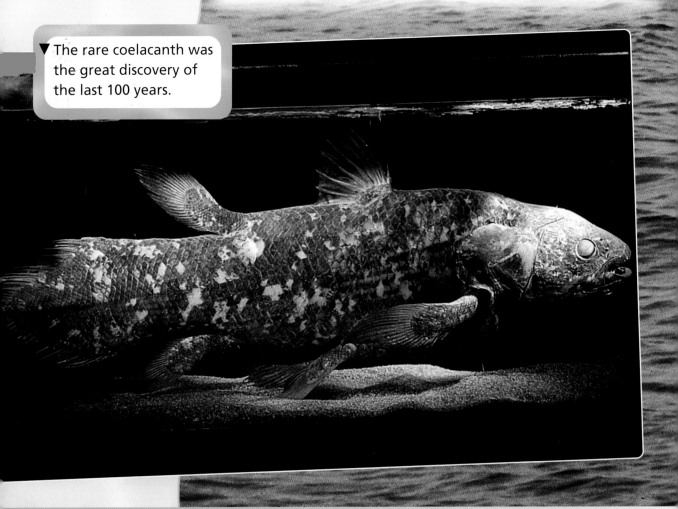

▼ The rare coelacanth was the great discovery of the last 100 years.

ancient   from a past age long ago
extinct   has died out, never to return

Top of the range

The marlin is related to the swordfish family. The swordfish's sharp bony jaw has been known to **pierce** wooden boats. Another super-fast member of the family is the sailfish (shown below). This has a large fin that sticks up like a huge sail on a boat.

▲ A marlin leaps from the sea with a remora fish hitching a fast ride.

Fastest

The blue marlin is sometimes called the sea-cheetah because it is such a fast hunter. It is built for speed with its super-**streamlined** shape. Its fins can fold away into grooves in its body to reduce any **friction**. This allows it to reach speeds of 80 kilometres (50 miles) per hour. The black marlin can be even faster and sometimes reaches 128 kilometres (80 miles) per hour. Its tough backbone and skeleton give its long tail extra power.

Marlin have long pointed noses like spears, which they use to slash through tuna fish. They tend to hunt alone in the open ocean. A marlin can grow to be 4 metres long and can live for about 20 years.

fossil   very old remains of living things found in mud and rock
pierce   stab or break through a surface

Bendy and big

You might think fish with soft, light and bendy skeletons cannot be very strong. Think again. Some of these fish are the biggest and toughest of all.

Rays

Of all the **cartilaginous** fish, the rays are the most gentle and graceful as well as strong. There are around 450 types of ray. They all 'fly' and glide gracefully along the sea-bed. Their wide fins flap slowly like a bird's wings. Some rays can grow to be over 4 metres across.

Most rays feed on shellfish and worms that they uncover on the sea-bed. When they need to hide, they lie still and cover themselves with sand. Manta rays often sweep up to the surface and at times leap out of the water in a somersault.

Secrets of the bat ray

This ray is dark brown with a white belly and large eyes. Its two long fins look like a bat's ears. Its flat body has a long, whip-like tail armed with a stinger. If stepped on or attacked, sting-rays can inject poison from their tail spines to kill their attacker. They may swim alone or in groups, as shown above.

cartilaginous   having soft bendy gristle rather than bone
prey   animal that is killed and eaten by other animals

Sharks

There are nearly 400 types of shark and all but a couple live in the sea. They do not have scales like other fish. In fact, their rough skin is covered with tiny pointed 'teeth'. If you stroke a shark the wrong way, it can even cut your skin.

Very few sharks are dangerous and some are even gentle and shy. One of these is the hammerhead shark. It is called this because of the strange shape of its flat head with eyes at each end. In fact, its head has thousands of tiny **receptors** along the edges. One is a scent **sensor** that tells the shark when **prey** is near. A direction sensor tells it how far away the prey is.

Hammerheads

These sharks can grow to be 4 metres long, but they very rarely attack humans. As with all sharks, they are in greater danger from us than we are from them. Hammerheads like the one on the left are caught mainly for the oil in their livers, which is rich in vitamin A. They feed on smaller sharks and fish buried in sand.

◄ Manta rays often rise to the surface of the ocean.

receptor   organ in the body that responds to a signal

Amazing bodies

Gills

Gills are feathery structures on the sides of a fish's head. Water comes in its mouth and passes out through the gill slits. The gills of a healthy fish are bright red because of the high level of oxygen in the many **blood vessels**. Without oxygen, the gills would be brown.

The big question that puzzled people for centuries was 'how do fish breathe?' If all life on our planet needs **oxygen** to **survive**, how do animals breathe where there is no air? The answer is that fish do not need air but they do need oxygen. There is plenty of oxygen in seas and rivers. At least, there should be.

Breathing

Just as we send air in and out of our nose and mouth all the time, fish keep gulping in water to pass out through their gills. Just like our lungs, the fish's gills take in oxygen and pass out **carbon dioxide**. And just like us, fish can 'drown' if they do not get the right mix of oxygen into their blood.

▲ These gills of an Atlantic salmon are healthy and red.

► Polluted water stops fish breathing so they soon die.

blood vessel　fine tube that carries blood all round the body
carbon dioxide　gas that animals breathe out

When fish cannot breathe

When small ponds dry up, all the fish crowd into the water that is left. If they use up all the oxygen in the water, they 'drown'. Fish can also drown if their gills are hurt in a fight.

If the oxygen supply in the water is getting very low, fish will rise to the surface. Bony fish can suck air at the surface into a sac-like organ called an air bladder. Some fish take oxygen out of this air instead of straight from the water. But when the surface of the water freezes in winter, the fish cannot reach that air and they may die.

Plants in water make oxygen. If **pollution** kills the plants, it will also kill the fish, as there will not be enough oxygen for them to breathe.

Newsflash: Herbert the Turbot!

One story shows how some fish can survive for hours without breathing.

Michael Reeves caught a 1 kilogram turbot in Dorset, England in 2002. He took it home and put in the fridge. Fifteen hours later the fish moved so he rushed it to a local aquarium. The cold fridge had slowed the fish down and kept it living. Today Herbert swims happily on show, alive and well.

pollution   spoiling natural things with dangerous chemicals or rubbish
survive   stay alive despite danger and difficulties

Lungfish

Every family has its odd one out. Fish have a very odd family member. The lungfish goes against all the rules of fish breathing because it has lungs as well as gills. This means it can behave strangely.

There are actually six **species** of lungfish known today. All six can breathe air when they need to. As well as using gills when they are swimming under water, they can go up to the surface and gulp down air. It means lungfish can leave the water and live on land.

These fish look like eels and live in lakes or rivers in Australia, South America and Africa. The South American lungfish can grow to over 1 metre. The African lungfish can reach over 2 metres in length.

Lungs and teeth

Even though lungfish can breathe air, it would not be wise to lift one out of the water. It would not harm the fish to be picked up, but it could be risky for the person. Lungfish will attack almost anything that moves, including human hands.

▲ It is best to keep lungfish in their own tank, as they are fearless and will attack anything.

slither   slip and slide along like a snake

Survival

The African lungfish has two lungs, which it uses when ponds dry up in the dry season. It buries itself in the mud and curls up. It makes extra slime that hardens to make a crust. The lungfish can then live through the dry season until the rain comes. When it gets wet again, the lungfish wakes up and **slithers** off to look for a pond. Scientists have even kept lungfish out of water for 4 years.

The Queensland lungfish of Australia has one lung. When its stream dries up, it pokes its head above the water to fill the lung. The sound it makes is said to be like a **wheezy** gasp! This lungfish can only **survive** a few days out of water.

Lungfish supper

Some people in Africa like to eat lungfish. How do people find them when they are buried deep in mud? It is easy. They pretend to be rain by tapping their fingers on the ground. The lungfish 'wake up' and think it is time to head for water.

▲ An African lungfish crawls across dry land.

wheezy   whistling chesty sound made when breathing

Living on land and water

Eels can be something of a mystery. There are nearly 700 different sorts. Some of them seem to look more like snakes or **amphibians** than fish. Yet fish they are – and most live on the sea-bed.

It is the eels that live in some lakes, ditches and rivers that do strange things. Some nights, they are on the move. They leave their fish world and become creatures of the land. They take **oxygen** from the air instead of from water. Just like amphibians, they can breathe through their skin without needing lungs. For years, people used to wonder how a new pond, miles from anywhere, suddenly became stocked with eels. Where did they come from? The answer is simple. The eels **slithered** miles all by themselves, breathing fresh air.

Land fish

Eels survive in almost any type of water, including salt, fresh, still or flowing. They live at the bottom of the water, under stones and in mud. Those that travel over land eat worms, insects or maybe the odd frog as they go.

► A European eel leaves its river to explore the land.

amphibian   cold-blooded animal that lives in water or on land
Everglades   a large area of swamp in Florida, USA

Common eel

The common eel can live out of water as long as it keeps cool and damp. By breathing through its skin, it takes in about half the amount of oxygen it would get from using its gills in water.

Asian swamp eel

The Asian swamp eel is more of a problem because it **survives** very well out of water. In the 1990s these eels somehow arrived in Florida. Ever since, they have been slithering across the **Everglades**, eating many small animals on their way. At 1 metre long, the swamp eel hides in swamps, ponds, canals, roadside ditches and rice fields. If the water dries up, it just slithers into mud or grass and lives there for months with no food.

Pests

Scientists have tried all sorts of ways to control the swamp eels in the Florida Everglades, shown above. Nothing really works. Poison does not affect them. Draining ponds is useless, as they would slither away somewhere else. Even explosives do not seem to harm them. They are tough fish!

---

oxygen   one of the gases in air and water that all living things need

Feeding

Cleaning up the sea floor

Cod feed by sucking up food on the sea-bed. In 2000, some Australian fishermen caught a cod that was about 1.5 metres long and cut it open. A man's head was in its stomach. Police thought the man had fallen into the sea and scavenging fish had eaten the body.

When it comes to feeding, there are four main types of fish.

- **Grazers** or plant eaters – such as parrotfish or grass carp.
- **Scavengers** that eat any waste matter on the sea-bed, including meat killed by other fish. Cod suck up all kinds of food in this way.
- Meat and insect eaters that kill their own food – such as mackerel.
- **Sifters** that eat tiny particles – such as basking sharks.

Grazing

Plant eaters tend to graze in shallow coastal waters where there is **algae** on the sea floor. They learn to scrape algae and sea urchins off rocks or nibble at seaweed.

Scavengers

The **sediment** on the ocean floor contains a lot of food. Scraps fall to the sea-bed and many fish simply pick up the pieces. They are the cleaners of the oceans.

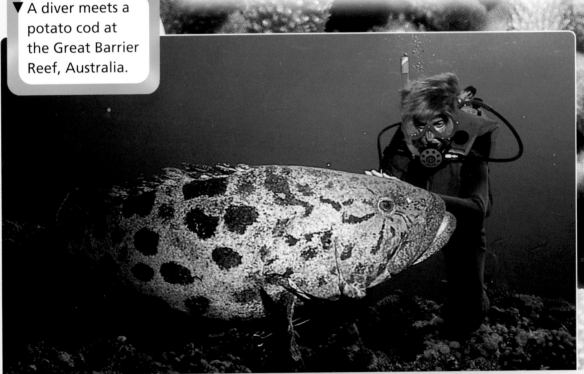

▼ A diver meets a potato cod at the Great Barrier Reef, Australia.

algae   types of simple plant without stems that grow in water or on rocks

Killers

Predators that kill other fish have to track down and chase their **prey**. Some lie in wait to ambush their food. Fish such as tuna travel long distances to search for food. Once they have found smaller fish, they need sharp teeth to eat them. **Carnivorous** fish have developed strong mouths to seize prey and swallow it whole or in large pieces.

Sifters

Filter feeders are fish that **sieve** food from water. Water is full of tiny particles of food. The fish suck in water and sift out the bits of food, such as very tiny animals or plant matter. Even some large sharks, such as whale sharks, feed like this. Although whales are **mammals**, many of them are also filter feeders. They eat very tiny animals called **krill**.

Can fish taste their food?

Even though fish gulp pieces of food down whole, they do have taste buds in and around the mouth. Fish such as catfish (above) have taste buds on their **barbels**. These are like whiskers round their mouths. They are used to find food.

◀ Grazing damsel fish pick algae from coral.

carnivorous   animal that eats other animals
sediment   matter that sinks to the bottom of the sea

Fish that bite

Some fish bite anything that looks like a passing meal. Sometimes it may be a human. One of the largest freshwater fish is the giant catfish. Some have been said to reach 3 metres long and weigh up to 250 kilograms. Stories tell of small dogs and ducks swimming quite happily until a giant catfish strikes. It will often swallow **prey** whole as it does not have sharp teeth for tearing. Because of this, some people fish for giant catfish by putting their hand down into a dark hole. They let the fish swallow their arm then scoop it out. Sometimes people have drowned by finding such a fish far too big to handle.

▲ Catfish may sense when they are in danger of being caught.

Pike

Some pike can grow to 1.5 metres. They live in rivers and eat fish, birds and small mammals – and sometimes people's fingers or toes. A Russian fisherman caught one and kissed it on the mouth. The fish bit his nose and would not let go – even when friends cut off the pike's head. The pike's head had to be removed at hospital.

▶ The snakefish is long enough to coil itself around. It is sometimes known as a ropefish.

mammal   warm-blood animal whose young feed on their mother's milk

Snakefish

The snakefish is like an eel, with a large mouth and sharp teeth. Some grow to over a metre long and they eat fish, frogs, birds and small **mammals**. They hit the news in the USA in 2002.

Another sighting of snakefish in the USA

Snakefish come from Asia and Africa but they have appeared in Crofton Pond, Maryland.

It seems a number were brought into the USA and let loose. The fish are described as looking like 'something from a bad horror movie'.

This **predator** fish can crawl over land and live out of water for a few days. It is thought they are also breeding in Lake Wylie in North Carolina. If so, they could soon empty the lake of all its other fish.

Stitches needed for tiger muskie victims

The largest pike (shown below) live in fresh water in North America. These muskies can weigh 30 kilograms. A metre-long tiger muskie took a bite from a 14-year-old boy's wrist in 1995. He had been swimming in Lake Rebecca, Minnesota. A similar muskie bit a chunk from a boy's foot in Twin Valley Lake, Wisconsin in 1998. He needed 60 stitches. So beware of muskies!

predator   animal that hunts and eats other animals

Piranha fact file

- There are over 20 different types of piranha fish.
- Only four types of piranha are thought to be of danger to humans.
- Some piranhas are **vegetarian**.
- Other piranhas are **cannibals** and will eat their own young.

Man-eaters of the river

Piranha fish have a bad name for killing people. In fact, these small fish are not always as deadly as some stories suggest. The name 'piranha' means 'tooth fish' or 'scissors'. That is because some do have little razor-sharp teeth. But they do not always attack. They can be quite safe.

Red-bellied piranhas are the more fearsome fish in this family. They can grow up to 36 centimetres long and can give quite a bite. They tend to swim in groups called a **shoal**. At times they become aggressive and look out for **prey** to attack. In the dry season the rivers lose water and the fish get hungry. They soon sense any blood in the water and that is when they seem to go crazy in a feeding **frenzy**.

► A shoal of piranha can soon put an end to a sick animal struggling in the water.

cannibal   animal that eats its own species
frenzy   wild fury or excitement

Eaten alive!

A few stories tell of people or animals falling into a river that quickly bubbles with thrashing piranhas. The fish strip the flesh from their **victim** in a matter of minutes. Such stories are quite rare and happen mostly in horror films. Even so, people who fish in rivers of South America have to be careful. Many have lost toes or fingers as they wade in the water. Red-bellied piranhas do an important job. They help to get rid of sick or weak animals that fall into the water. They clean up the river and can even stop disease spreading.

Bigger man-eater

Bull sharks like the one below can live in the sea and in rivers. They have been known to swim for miles up rivers in South Africa. Some have even attacked small boats. These 3-metre-long sharks are known for killing a few people each year. They are also called Zambezi sharks.

shoal   group of fish – sometimes called a 'school'
vegetarian   animal that does not eat meat – sometimes called a herbivore

The biggest

The biggest great white shark to be caught was a female. It was 6.4 metres long and was caught in 1945 in the sea off Cuba. It weighed 3312 kilograms and was 4.5 metres around its middle.

Man-eaters of the sea

There may be around 100 attacks on people each year from all types of sharks. Less than half of these attacks will kill someone. Yet people kill about 100 million sharks each year. This can be for sport, for food or just to keep beaches 'shark free' for tourists.

Great white sharks

The great white shark attacks more people than any other shark. Great whites simply bite things to see if they are worth eating. Sometimes they bite surfers who look like seals to the sharks below. Then it is soon on the TV. News reports and films such as *Jaws* make us think the great white shark is the all-time big bad fish.

◄ Sharks lose and grow their teeth throughout their life.

fatal   causing death

Tiger sharks

The next shark the world loves to hate is the tiger shark. Again, this shark attacks just a few people each year. It is usually 3–4 metres long, but some have reached over 7 metres. The tiger shark has a blunt snout and stripes on its back. It lives in warm seas around the world and tends to swim near the surface. It can reach speeds of 32 kilometres (20 miles) per hour and can travel up to 80 kilometres (50 miles) a day.

Tiger sharks rely on their keen sense of smell to detect **prey**. They will eat almost anything, including seals, turtles, sea birds, fish, sea snakes, other sharks and rubbish. Fishermen have found all sorts inside tiger sharks, such as bottles, cans, car number plates, tyres, ships' anchors …
and bits of humans!

Great barracuda

They call the barracuda (shown above) 'the tiger of the sea' as it is a fierce hunter in the Caribbean. It can reach 1.8 metres in length and weigh 40 kilograms, and it has savage teeth. Although not really man-eaters, giant barracudas have given humans nasty wounds. These are not **fatal**, but they usually need stiches.

◄ The stripes give tiger sharks their name.

prey   animal that is killed and eaten by other animals

Gentle giants

As the biggest known fish in the world, the whale shark can look scary. In fact these large sharks have a gaping mouth because they are feeding all the time. They need to, because they weigh as much as six elephants. They have huge mouths up to 1.4 metres wide. Their skin can be 10 centimetres thick, the thickest skin of any living animal. They live in deep, warm seas and often **cruise** near the surface.

Whale sharks are filter feeders. They swim slowly, sucking up water full of **plankton** and tiny fish. They pump the filtered water out through their gills. Whale sharks usually stay on their own and just meet in groups now and again. They swim gently and are harmless to humans.

Plankton – the sea's life-line

Plankton forms the base of the **food chain** in the ocean. Many **species** feed on this 'soup' of tiny particles that float in the sea. Plankton is made up of **microscopic** plants and animals and tiny eggs of crabs or fish such as herring. The picture above shows plankton highly magnified.

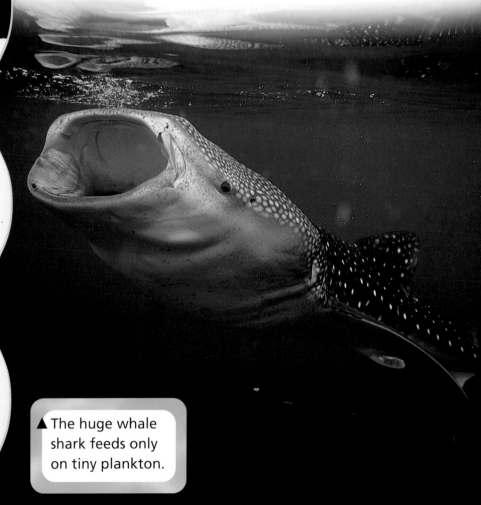

▲ The huge whale shark feeds only on tiny plankton.

cruise   travel gently, with no rush
food chain   order in which one living thing feeds on another

▼ Large basking sharks often feed off the Cornish coast in the UK.

Basking sharks

Basking sharks are the next biggest fish in the world. Some weigh about 4 tonnes. The largest recorded basking shark was 12.3 metres long. On average, females are about 9 metres and males are nearly 7 metres long. They live in the Atlantic and Pacific oceans and are seen off European coasts.

Like whale sharks, basking sharks drift slowly through the sea with their huge mouths filtering out plankton. They may take in about 1.5 million litres of water an hour. Five thousand slits in their gills strain the food. In winter, they lose these so they cannot feed during this time. These huge sharks sometimes gather in large groups of 100 or more. When young are born, they are 1.5 metres long.

Krill

Krill are one of the most important food sources in the ocean. They are tiny shrimp-like animals that drift in their millions in the sea. Filter feeders eat many tonnes of this **protein**-rich food every day. Scientists think that all the krill in the ocean (650 million tonnes) would weigh more than all the humans on Earth.

plankton   tiny plants, eggs and animals that drift in the sea
protein   nutrient in food that is used by the body for growth and repair

Breeding

Like all animals, fish have a strong **instinct** to increase the number of their **species**. They spend a lot of energy finding a mate to make and raise young fish.

Reproduction

So many things affect how often different fish breed. Light, heat, tides and food supply are all important in **reproduction**. So is the water itself. **Pollution** not only harms eggs, it can also make fish change sex. This can mean a species may stop breeding altogether.

Meeting

Fish use many tricks to attract a mate. Some perform all kinds of dancing displays while others show off bright colours. In the deep sea, where it is dark, fish like the lanternfish light up to say, 'I am yours!'

▲ Female splash tetra lay eggs on leaves. Males flick water to keep the eggs wet.

Mating

The usual way that fish breed is for the male to **fertilize** the female's eggs by moving beside her and releasing **sperm** as she releases her eggs. Some females, like guppies and sharks, keep the eggs inside their bodies. The young hatch inside and are born live into the water. Some fish eggs may take just one day to hatch. Others take up to many months.

► Lantern fish use lights to find each other in the dark, deep water.

instinct   fixed way of behaving that comes naturally
fertilize   when a sperm joins an egg and makes a new individual

Looking after the family

The male three-spine stickleback builds a nest out of weed to attract a female. He glues it together by a sort of cement made by his kidneys.

The female splash tetra of South America lays her eggs on leaves by leaping out of the river. The male then leaps out to fertilize them. He keeps the eggs wet by splashing them with his tail until they hatch.

Some bony fish are both sexes in one. A single fish makes both sperm and eggs. Some fish of the wrasse family are born female and later become male. Some damselfish are born as males and change into females. Sea bass can change from female to male and then back again. Being a fish can be very confusing!

Can you believe it?

The mola mola or ocean sunfish lays up to 50 million eggs at one time. Cod can lay a mere 8 million. If they all **survived**, the sea would be packed with fish. Some sharks, however, only produce a few eggs at a time.

▲ These Californian sunfish produce a vast amount of eggs.

reproduction   producing more of the same species
sperm   male sex cell

Struggle

Fish ladders (shown on the right, below) are often used in rivers where salmon swim. People put them by **dams** in the rivers to help salmon get back to their spawning grounds. Each female salmon lays 2500 to 7000 eggs. Very few eggs will ever become an adult that can have young itself.

Spawning salmon

The way some salmon **spawn** is one of the wonders of nature. Atlantic and Pacific salmon sense the right time to leave the sea. They swim thousands of miles up rivers to breed. They head for the exact stream in the hills where they once hatched. Their journey is full of danger as they struggle upstream. Sometimes they have to leap up waterfalls and avoid **predators** such as bears and eagles.

Those salmon that make it 'home' dig a nest in the gravel. The female lays her eggs and the male **fertilizes** them. By now, the starved Pacific salmon are so worn out that they soon die. Their eggs must **survive** without them.

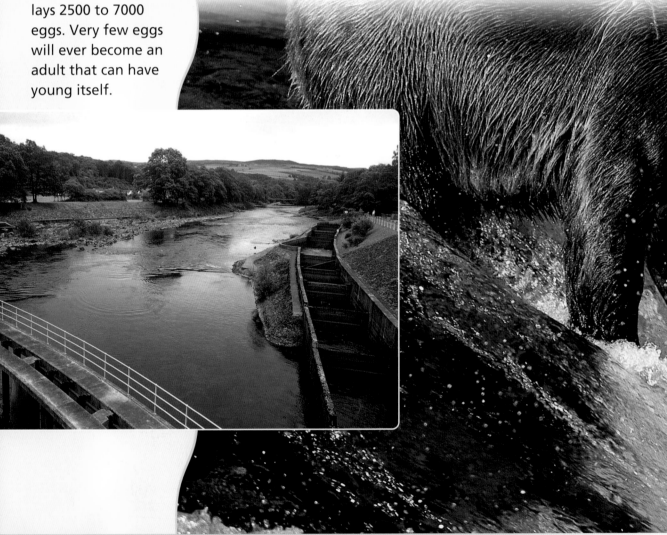

abdomen   middle part of the body around the stomach
dam   wall built to hold back water

New life

The newly hatched young salmon stay buried in the gravel nest. They feed on stores of **nutrients** from egg yolk attached to their **abdomen**. When all the yolk has gone, the young salmon leave the nest. They now begin to eat tiny plants and insects.

Soon the small fish begin their long journey downstream to the sea. Many will not survive because other fish will eat them. Those salmon that make it to the sea will live there and grow for up to 4 years. Some will reach over a metre long and weigh as much as 30 kilograms. At last, it is time for them to swim towards their birthplace and spawn.

The eel's story

Freshwater eels live in rivers and lakes but they travel thousands of miles to spawn at sea. American and European eels breed in the Sargasso Sea near Florida in the USA. Years after hatching, the small eels swim up rivers to where they grow. Then it is back to sea to spawn and die.

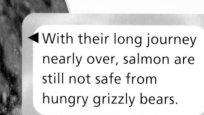

◄ With their long journey nearly over, salmon are still not safe from hungry grizzly bears.

spawn   lay eggs in water and fertilize them

Did you know?

- Baby seahorses must rise to the surface to gulp air when they are born. This air fills their **swim bladder** and lets them float.

- The common seahorse of the Atlantic coast of North America grows to over 13 centimetres in length. The Pacific seahorse can grow to 30 centimetres.

Strange parents

The most unusual fish when it comes to producing young must be the seahorse. The parents go against all the rules. It is the father who gives birth. The mother does not have much to do with the babies at all.

Seahorses tend to be partners for life. The female lays 100–200 eggs inside a pouch on the front of the male. She does this by dropping the eggs through a tube put into his pouch. The male lets **sperm** into his pouch and the eggs are **fertilized**. For a few weeks the young seahorses grow inside his pouch. He feeds them with juices made by his body.

▶ Most young seahorses take a year to mature.

swim bladder   air sac inside bony fish that stops them from sinking

Birth

The time comes for the male seahorse to give birth. It can take him 2 days and he seems worn out afterwards. His pouch begins to squeeze the young seahorses and push them out. Clumps of young fish shoot out from his pouch. Some are only 1 centimetre long. As soon as they are born, the small seahorses begin to look after themselves.

Although seahorses keep their partner for life, some female seahorses may have more eggs than the male's pouch will carry. In that case, she looks for a second male to carry the rest of her eggs. If a male still has room left in his pouch for more eggs, he will mate with another female to fill his pouch.

Pipefish

Like its cousin the seahorse, the pipefish (shown above) has a long snout and no teeth. The male keeps the eggs in his pouch before he gives birth.

The largest pipefish grow to about 50 centimetres long.

◀ Baby seahorses are being born from this male seahorse's pouch.

Defence

It is not easy being a small fish. Everyone wants to eat you! Many fish have developed all kinds of ways to stay alive in a hungry world.

Kill or cure

The electric torpedo ray (shown below) gives shocks to its prey from fins near each eye. In Roman times doctors used to strap a live ray to a patient's head. It was meant to cure a headache!

Electric

Some fish have a special weapon – electricity. Even though this power is used to help fish find their way around, it can also come in very handy when they are under attack. A few fish make an **electric field** and use special **sensors** along their body. These 'read' what is going on around them. It is like getting lots of quick photo images back.

Sea water **conducts** electricity better than fresh water so fish in the sea do not have to make very much electricity. Even so, a torpedo ray can give out 220 volts. That is enough to give you a real shock.

Wild words   **aquarium**   place containing tanks of living fish
                   conduct   transmit energy

Livewires

Electric eels live in rivers in South America. They can shoot out over 600 volts of electricity or sometimes as much as 800 volts. That is enough to kill a horse. It could be **fatal** for a person standing on an electric eel. The fish has electric cells in its tail that slowly charge up like a big battery. This energy helps to guide the eel in murky water. And that is where it is easy to step on one. The eel uses these shock tactics to stun its **prey** and also to harm any attacker.

The stargazer fish is in the perch family. It lies in wait in sand to stun any passing prey using electric organs between its eyes. If something tries to eat it, it must be like chewing a live wire.

High voltage

The electric catfish lives in Africa and can grow to over a metre long. It can give a quick zap of up to 350 volts of electricity to stun prey or keep **predators** away. It also seems to respond to **currents** in the Earth a few hours before an earthquake strikes.

▼ Some electric eels can grow to almost 3 metres long.

▼ An electric catfish can only share an **aquarium** with its own young. Any other fish would die of shock.

current   movement of electrical energy
electric field   area affected by electrical energy

The lion-fish

The lion-fish belongs to the deadly scorpion-fish family. It has poisonous spines. People can get a nasty jab but they usually **survive**, in spite of the great pain. The venom in the spines remains active for days. Lion-fish live on the Great Barrier Reef in Australia.

Poison

The best way small fish can stop bigger fish eating them is to taste horrible or to be deadly. In fact, some small fish can even kill people with their **venom**. One of these is the stonefish, which grows to 35 centimetres. Its venom can be deadly. It lies on the sea-bed with spikes sticking up to stop sharks from eating it. But if a person steps on one, it can be very dangerous. These fish live in the sea off northern Australia.

Surgeonfish defend themselves by being sharp like knives. Spikes tipped with venom flick out from their tails when they are under threat. They can give people nasty cuts but nothing worse. These fish can be 20–100 centimetres long and come from Hawaii.

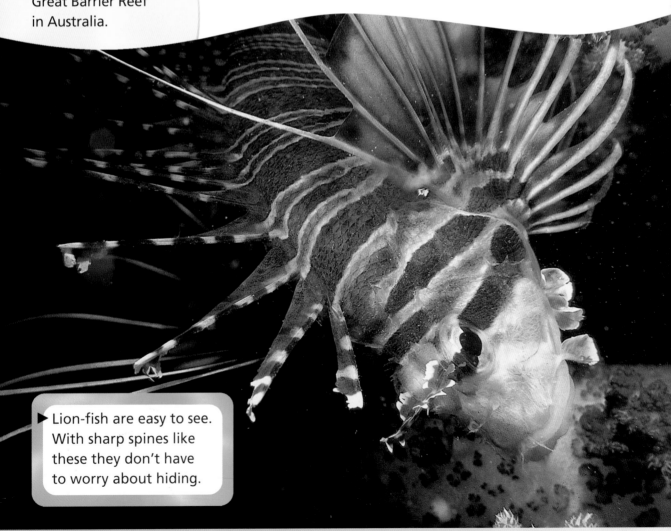

▶ Lion-fish are easy to see. With sharp spines like these they don't have to worry about hiding.

antidote   medicine that will act against a poison
gene   part of a cell that controls how that individual grows

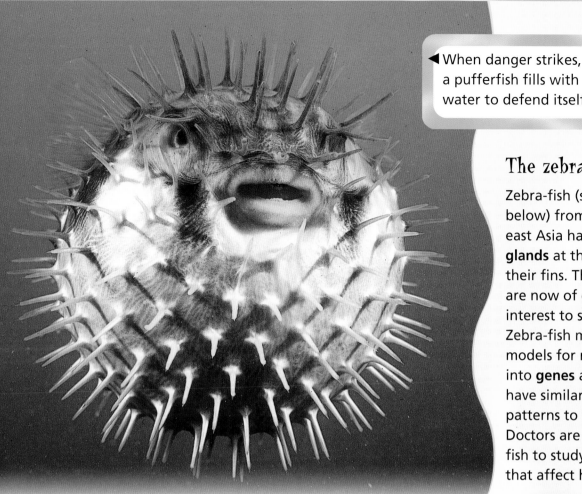

◄ When danger strikes, a pufferfish fills with water to defend itself.

The zebra-fish

Zebra-fish (shown below) from South-east Asia have poison **glands** at the base of their fins. These fish are now of great interest to science. Zebra-fish make ideal models for research into **genes** as they have similar gene patterns to humans. Doctors are using this fish to study diseases that affect humans.

The pufferfish

The pufferfish is so-called because when it is threatened, it puffs up to about twice its normal size by gulping water. Pufferfish range in size from just a few centimetres long to almost 60 centimetres. There are 100 different sorts that live in the Pacific and Indian oceans. When it puffs up like a ball, a pufferfish can swim at only about half its normal speed. But it does not have to hurry. Its spines stick out like a porcupine's. Nothing would try to swallow that. Even if it did, the poison inside the fish could be deadly. Some of its organs are full of poison. Even cooking does not make the fish safe. People have died from eating it, as there is no known **antidote**.

gland part of the body that makes chemicals and other substances
venom poison

Hide and seek

One way to keep away from hungry mouths is to hide inside a safe one – mum's mouth! Some fish are called mouthbrooders because the mother protects her eggs and young by holding them in her mouth. One sign of trouble and in they all go!

Camouflage

Another way to avoid being eaten is by using **camouflage**. Many fish seem **invisible** when their colour matches their background. Others have stripes that break up their shape and make them harder to see. Some fish look like stones or weed. And others can turn to one side and almost disappear because they are flat. Such camouflage is a life-saver.

Flatfish

Flatfish cannot swim fast but they can squeeze into cracks to escape. They can also lie flat on the sea-bed and no one will know they are there. They have both eyes on one side of their body. Some, like the sculpin and flounder, can change colour to match the sand. Others just cover themselves in sand and lie flat until danger has passed.

▲ In some **species** of mouthbrooder, the male may look after the young.

coral reef   ridge in warm seas made of the skelectons of millions of tiny sea animals

Moray eels

Moray eels hide in nooks and crannies in rocks. Only their eyes can be seen as they wait for a passing fish supper. At the same time, larger fish cannot see or get at the moray in its little den. Chain morays live in the shallow reefs and rocky coastlines of the Caribbean. Their golden, chain-like patterns camouflage their movements as they **slither** around in search of crabs.

Stonefish

Lying on the sea-bed, the Australian stonefish has perfect camouflage and looks just like a crusty rock. It feeds on small fish and shrimps. When they swim by, the stonefish opens its mouth and gulps them down in less than a second.

Smelly camouflage

Some of the 80 species of parrotfish (above) have an interesting trick to defend themselves. They camouflage their smell at night so they can sleep safely in **coral reefs**. They cover themselves with a jelly-like substance that stops their enemies from 'sniffing them out' to eat them.

◀ When a plaice lies still on the sea-bed, no one is likely to see it.

invisible   not able to be seen

Weird and wonderful

Fish behave in weird and wonderful ways but some are extraordinary. They do things that other fish just would not attempt.

Fish that fly

Some fish can leave the water and seem to fly. In fact, a flying fish glides rather than flies. It leaps out of the sea with its fins folded and then spreads them like wings. It skims over the water as its tail beats down to give it speed and to lift the fish clear of the surface. A single glide can take a fish 180 metres over the sea. Flying fish use this trick for when they need to make a quick escape. Sometimes it takes them into worse danger. Often flying fish fly right onto the decks of ships, where they get stranded.

Record

A flying fish **vibrates** its tail over 50 beats per second to get enough speed for take-off. The flying fish's record is a distance of over 200 metres. In a few glides it can keep flying for over 40 seconds.

► Flying fish leave a trail in the water as they skim the surface of the sea.

vibrate   quiver or move to and fro very quickly

So why do flying fish fly instead of swim? Simple – it is faster. Air gives less **friction** than water so the flying fish can escape from dolphins, tuna or other fast **predators** far more quickly. They simply leap across the surface of the sea.

Flying fish hit round-the-world sailors

RIO DE JANEIRO, Brazil – March 2002

Boats in the Volvo Ocean Race have braved a giant **waterspout** in the Sydney–Hobart race. They have had to cope with icebergs and storms in the Southern Ocean. But now, in the Caribbean, they have been battered by flying fish. Sailors are being hit as the 25-centimetre 'winged wonders' leap out of the water at 64 kilometres (40 miles) per hour. A number of sailors have been thumped in the chest and knocked over as the fish crash into them.

Danger

Some fish that leap out of the sea have caused nasty accidents. A man named Anthony Fernando was reported to have been killed by a garfish (below) off the coast of Sri Lanka in 1988. The fish, like a swordfish, leaped from the sea and speared his neck.

---

waterspout   twisting column of water and spray like a whirlwind over the sea

Sticking together

Some fish have a special arrangement with other fish that suits both partners. At least 45 **species** have a deal with bigger fish that they keep clean.

One of the busiest cleaners of the sea is the cleaner wrasse. In fact, it often has **clients** lining up to be cleaned. The wrasse eats all sorts of **parasites** from the gills and even the mouths of large **carnivores**. The bigger fish just let the wrasse munch away – all round their deadly teeth and gums.

But another little fish has learned to copy the wrasse. It is called a 'false cleaner' and while the bigger fish happily lets it nibble away, the false wrasse suddenly bites a chunk from its client's fins. A dirty trick!

Dangerous friend

The remora fish helps to keep sharks clean by picking off parasites. It hitches a ride and sticks close to the shark's side, as shown below. The shark pays it back by being a **permanent** bodyguard and agreeing not to bite. The remora gets to eat the shark's leftovers, too.

client   customer
permanent   lasting for a very long time

Doctor fish

Another fish likes to nibble away at the dead scales and skin of other animals. The bigger fish are happy to let the kangal fish of Turkey do its job. It is a member of the carp family and it is very good at giving a sort of massage. In fact, it is sometimes called the doctor fish.

It can do humans a lot of good, too. These fish have helped people with skin problems. As they pick at scabs and sores, the fish can help to heal diseased skin. The patient just has to sit in a tub full of kangal fish and let them nibble. It might seem scary, but many people are certain it helps them to get better.

Safe

The clown fish (above) coats itself with slime. This protects it from the stinging **tentacles** of the **sea anemone** where it lives. That means other fish cannot get to the clown fish to eat it. The anemone could live without the clown fish – but not the other way round.

 A wrasse hops into a coral trout's mouth for a quick brush and polish!

Hot and cold

The pupfish lives in hot springs in California, USA where the water temperature is a steaming 40 °C. Meanwhile, the Alaska blackfish lives in ponds and streams in freezing Alaska. It can **survive** for 30 minutes in temperatures as low as –20 °C.

Jawless suckers

Some people go swimming in rivers and the sea and come out covered in blood-sucker fish. These fish live by feeding off others. Hagfish and lampreys are such **parasites**. They do not have jaws but a mouth that sucks on to another fish. River lampreys suck out the blood and juices of any fish they can find. Sometimes three or four lampreys could be stuck on one fish. A number of different types live in rivers in the USA. Do not worry – lampreys are only small. If they suck on to a human, they can be pulled off.

A single lamprey can suck and kill as many as 18 kilograms of fish in a year. That is a big problem to the fish stocks of the Great Lakes and Chesapeake Bay, USA.

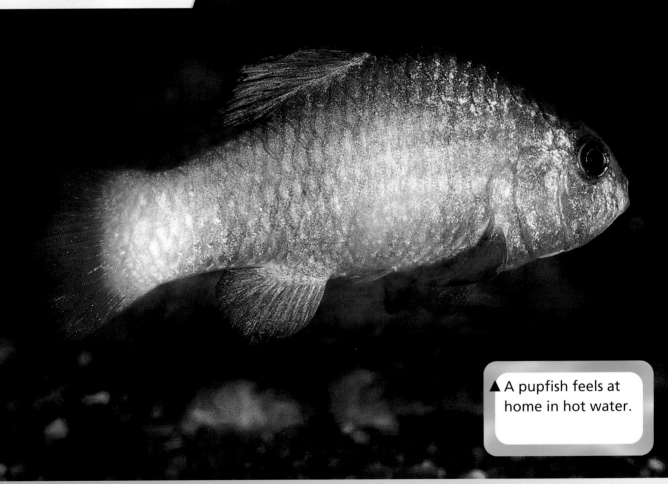

▲ A pupfish feels at home in hot water.

indigestion   pain and difficulty in digesting food

The deep

Then there is the weird world in the deep, dark sea. Some amazing fish live kilometres down in the Pacific Ocean. We still do not know about many of them.

Strange anglerfish have their own 'rod and line' to catch other fish. This hangs over the anglerfish's head. When the end lights up, fish are drawn to it. All the anglerfish has to do is open its mouth and eat the fish.

The hairy anglerfish is covered in spines that pick up vibrations in the water. This helps them to find **prey** in the dark. The 'hairy angler' just opens its huge mouth, filled with teeth. Its stomach can swell so much that it can swallow prey larger than itself.

Moray eel facts

- **Ancient** Romans bred moray eels in seaside ponds and are thought to have fed them on live slaves who were no good.

- There are about 80 **species** of moray eel and their flesh can be **toxic**. King Henry I of England (1068–1135) was meant to have died from **indigestion** caused by eating a moray eel.

◄ In deep, dark waters, prey can only see the light on the angler fish's rod. It's just as well they can't see its face!

toxic   poisonous

Fish in danger

The Great Barrier Reef

The Great Barrier Reef, off Australia's east coast, is home to more than 1500 species of fish, 4000 types of mollusc and more than 200 species of bird. At over 1600 kilometres (1000 miles) long, this reef is the biggest structure ever built by living things. It can be seen clearly from space, as shown below – stretched across the dark blue sea.

Like many places on Earth, our oceans are at risk. They are changing fast.

Coral reefs

About a third of all fish **species** live in **coral reefs**. Maybe up to 3 million animal species like **molluscs**, jellyfish, starfish and **crustaceans** shelter and feed on coral reefs. Coral reefs are one of the richest **habitats** on Earth, but they only make up 1 per cent of the oceans.

Coral is made up of the skeletons of a tiny jelly-like animal with **tentacles**. It is like a very small **sea anemone**. Each tiny animal, called a polyp, joins with others to make forests of coloured coral reefs. When they die, the coral turns white. Coral reefs are under great threat from **pollution**. It is feared that only 30 per cent of today's coral reefs will remain in 50 years.

crustacean   animal with jointed legs and a hard shell, such as a shrimp or lobster
exhaustion   tired to the point of collapse

Seahorses under threat

Coral reefs are full of life and are rich in food. Some of the most colourful **shoals** of fish live on reefs. Reefs are also the home to species of brightly coloured seahorses. Seahorses fix themselves to the coral with their tails and wait for prawns to swim by. To catch them, the seahorse just straightens its tail and rises up. The small fins on its back push it through the water. But rough waves can tear seahorses off the coral and they soon die of **exhaustion**.

Humans are the biggest threat to the coral's seahorses. Twenty million seahorses are harvested each year for making traditional medicines. The world seahorse population has dropped by 50 per cent in the last 10 years. These amazing animals are now at great risk.

Colour under the sea

The warm, light, shallow water where corals grow is just right for **algae**. Algae grows on the coral and helps it to harden. Many species feed off the algae, like the brightly coloured mandarin fish shown above. Fish in the coral reefs are full of colour.

◄ Coral reefs support a mass of colourful fish of all sizes. Some divers say the moving shoals of fish look like liquid rainbows.

habitat   natural home of an animal
mollusc   soft-bodied animal without a backbone and often with a shell

Threat

The southern bluefin tuna is one of the largest bony fish in the world at over 4 metres long. It has been so heavily fished that it is nearly extinct. The flesh has a high fat content and is prized in Japan. One large fish weighing up to 900 kilograms can fetch over US $10,000.

Endangered fish

The spotted handfish is one of the world's most **endangered** sea fish. This pear-shaped fish has fins like hands that allow it to 'walk' along the sea floor. It is cream in colour with yellow-brown spots. The pattern on each fish is **unique** – just like fingerprints. Like the anglerfish, the spotted handfish has a small **lure** just above its mouth. But it does not seem to use this to attract prey so the purpose is a mystery.

Spotted handfish were quite common in Tasmania until the 1980s. Just two were seen between 1990 and 1994. By 2001, there were only three breeding groups. The arrival of the Northern Pacific seastar fish into this area may be the problem. The seastar is a **predator** and eats the handfish's eggs.

endangered   in danger of becoming extinct
lure   thing used to attract – like bait to a fish

Sturgeon

The Baltic sturgeon can reach 3.5 metres in length, but it is not the fish itself that people want to eat when they catch it. The sturgeon's eggs are used to make caviar. The USA is the world's biggest caviar importer. People can pay $100 for just 50 grams. Sturgeon can lay millions of sticky eggs at one time but they have now been fished until they are almost **extinct**. So many eggs are taken to make caviar that now very few fish are hatching. Today it is a **protected species**.

The largest sturgeon in the world is the Beluga. It grows to 5 metres in length and is the rarest sturgeon of all. It is the most expensive fish in the world, but there are now hardly any left in Russia's Caspian Sea.

Very rare

In just one river cave in Namibia, Africa, there are a few very rare catfish. These cave catfish (shown below) lack colour because their world is so dark. They are a pale pinkish white and look a bit like an eel. Their eyes are either very tiny or covered with skin. They are in danger if the water level drops in the cave, as the **species** will disappear forever.

◄ The spotted handfish is now so rare it is a protected species.

protected species   animals that it is against the law to harm or kill
unique   there is only one of its kind

Over-fishing

Bluefin tuna are one of the most valuable fish in the sea. Eighty thousand tonnes were caught every year in the early 1960s. The number of adult bluefins in the Western Atlantic is thought to have dropped almost 90 per cent since 1970. They may not survive long into the 21st century.

Save our seas

There is no doubt that many fish are under great threat today. Our rivers and oceans are in more danger now than at any time. Over 97 per cent of all life on Earth lives in the oceans, which affect the health and survival of all living things. But one of the biggest problems today is over-fishing. Fish give humans the greatest supply of the world's **protein**, but too much is being taken out of the sea. Many fish are caught before they are old enough to breed, so no young are replacing them. We take out tonnes of fish each day and replace them with tonnes of rubbish. We are slowly poisoning our seas.

► Oil slicks from tankers endanger life in and on the oceans.

global warming   warming up of the Earth due to burning fossil fuels such as coal and oil

Sea dangers

Stocks of Atlantic cod and haddock are now very low.
Bluefin tuna has also been over-fished round the world.
In the next few years we are in danger of losing some **species**
of fish forever unless we take more care. **Pollution** from
oil-spills and chemical run-offs from the land poison the
water where fish breed.

Drilling for oil, **whaling** and using fishing nets that tangle up
too many species are putting all fish in danger. **Global warming**
and dumping of waste in the sea are killing off the **coral reefs**.
So we need to act now to save our oceans and the fantastic fish
that share our planet – in their incredible underwater world.

What can we do?

- Take an interest
  in what is going
  on in our oceans.
  Find out which
  organizations are
  at work and what
  they are doing
  nearest to you.

- See how
  organizations
  like the Ocean
  Conservancy
  suggest you might
  get involved.

- Think 'green' by
  saving energy,
  cutting down waste
  and recycling. It
  all makes for a
  healthier planet.

whaling   hunting and killing of whales

Find out more

Organizations

BBC Nature
Website packed with games and quizzes to find out about all aspects of science.
bbc.co.uk/nature

Ecowatch
Website with photos and information about all sorts of incredible creatures.
ento.csiro.au/Ecowatch

Natural History Museum
Website includes online interactive exhibits.
nhm.ac.uk/interactive

Books

Classifying Fish, Richard and Louise Spilsbury (Heinemann Library, 2003)
From Egg to Adult: The Life Cycle of Fish, Richard and Louise Spilsbury (Heinemann Library, 2003)
Killer Creatures: Shark, Tony Allan and David Jefferis (Belitha, 2002)
Weird Wildlife: Sea Creatures, Clare Oliver (Belitha, 2002)
Wild Predators! Killer Fish, Andrew Solway (Heinemann Library, 2004)

World Wide Web

If you want to find out more about fish, you can search the Internet using keywords like these:

- fish
- amazing + fish
- 'puffer fish'

You can also find your own keywords by using headings or words from this book. Use the following search tips to help you find the most useful websites.

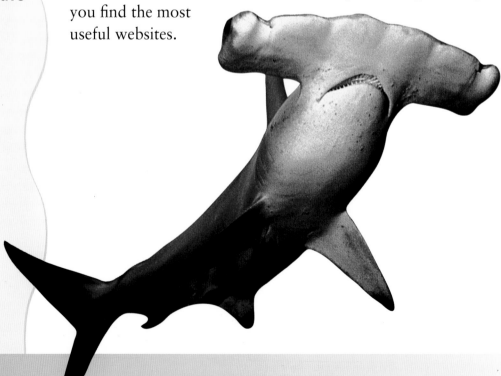

Search tips

There are billions of pages on the Internet so it can be difficult to find exactly what you are looking for.

For example, if you just type in 'water' on a search engine like Google, you will get a list of 50 million web pages. These search skills will help you find useful websites more quickly:

- Use simple keywords instead of whole sentences
- Use two to six keywords in a search, putting the most important words first
- Be precise – only use names of people, places or things
- If you want to find words that go together, put quote marks around them
- Use the advanced section of your search engine
- Use the + sign between keywords to link them. For example, typing + KS3 after your keyword will help you find web pages at the right level.

Where to search

Search engine
A search engine looks through a small proportion of the web and lists all sites that match the words in the search box. It can give thousands of links, but the best matches are at the top of the list, on the first page.
Try bbc.co.uk/search

Search directory
A search directory is like a library of websites that have been sorted by a person instead of a computer. You can search by keyword or subject and browse through the different sites like you look through books on a library shelf.
A good example is yahooligans.com

Numbers of incredible creatures

Creatures (y-axis): Amphibians, Mammals, Reptiles, Birds, Fish, Arachnids, Molluscs, Insects

Number of species (approximate) (x-axis): 0, 20,000, 40,000, 60,000, 80,000, 100,000, 120,000, 140,000, 160,000, 180,000, 1,000,000

Glossary

abdomen part of the body containing the stomach

algae types of simple plant without stems that grow in water or on rocks

amphibian cold-blooded animal that lives in water or on land

ancient from a past age long ago

antidote medicine to make a poison safe

aquarium place containing tanks of living fish

barbels body parts like long whiskers that grow from the mouth of some fish

blood vessel fine tube that carries blood all round the body

camouflage colour that matches the background

cannibal animal that eats its own species

carbon dioxide gas that animals breathe out

carnivore meat-eater

cartilaginous having soft bendy gristle rather than bone

client customer

conduct transmit energy

coral reef ridge in warm seas made of the skeletons of millions of tiny sea animals

cruise travel gently, with no rush

crustacean animal with jointed legs and a hard shell, such as a crab or lobster

current movement of electrical energy

dam wall built to hold back water

electric field area affected by electrical energy

endangered at risk of disappearing forever

environment natural surroundings or habitat

Everglades large area of swamp in Florida, USA

exhaustion tired to the point of collapse

extinct has died out, never to return

fatal causing death

fertilize when a sperm joins an egg and makes a new individual

food chain order in which one living thing feeds on another

fossil very old remains of things that onced lived, found in mud and rock

frenzy wild fury or excitement

friction drag or force when things rub together

gene information in living things that tells how they will grow

gland part of the body that makes hormones and other substances

global warming warming up of the Earth due to burning fossil fuels such as coal and oil

grazer any animal that feeds only on plants like grass or sea grass

habitat natural home of an animal

indigestion pain and difficulty in digesting food

instinct fixed way of behaving that comes naturally

invisible not able to be seen

krill tiny shrimp-like animals that swim in large numbers in the sea

lure thing used to attract – like bait to a fish

mammal warm-blooded animal that has hair and feeds its young on milk

microscopic can only be seen using an instrument that magnifies tiny objects

mollusc soft-bodied animal without a backbone and often with a shell

nutrient important substance found in food and needed by the body

oxygen one of the gases in air and water that all living things need

parasite animal or plant that lives in or on another living thing

permanent lasting for a very long time

pierce stab or break through a surface

plankton tiny plants, eggs and animals that drift in the sea

pollution spoiling natural things with dangerous chemicals or rubbish

predator animal that hunts and eats other animals

prey animal that is killed and eaten by other animals

propel drive or push forward

protected species animals that it is against the law to harm or kill

protein nutrient in food that is used by the body for growth and repair

receptor organ in the body that responds to a signal

reproduction producing more of the same species

reptile group of cold-blooded animals with scales, such as snakes and lizards

scavenger animal that feeds off scraps and the prey of others

sea anemone sea animal that attaches itself to a rock

sediment matter that sinks to the bottom of the sea

sensor device that detects and measures a type of signal

shoal group of fish – sometimes called a 'school'

sieve sift out solids from a liquid

sifter fish that sucks in water and filters out all the small bits of food

slither slip and slide along like a snake

spawn lay eggs in water and fertilize them

species type of living animal or plant

sperm male sex cell

streamlined torpedo-shaped

survive stay alive despite danger and difficulties

swim bladder air sac inside bony fish that stops them from sinking

tentacle body part that is like a long thin arm

toxic poisonous

unique there is only one of its kind

vegetarian animal that does not eat meat – sometimes called a herbivore

venom poison

vertebrate any animal that has a skeleton with a backbone

vibrate quiver or move to and fro very quickly

victim animal that gets hurt or killed

waterspout twisting column of water and spray like a whirlwind over the sea

whaling hunting and killing of whales

wheezy whistling, chesty sound made when breathing

Index

anglerfish 45

barracuda 25
bendy fish 4, 5, 10
blood-sucker fish 44
bony fish 4, 5, 13, 29

camouflage 7, 38–9
carnivorous fish 18, 19,
    20–3, 42
catfish 19, 20, 35, 49
clown fish 43
cod 18, 29, 51
coelacanth 8
coral reefs 46–7, 51

eels 16–17, 31, 35, 39, 45
electricity 34–5

filter feeders 19, 26, 27
fins 6, 9, 10
flatfish 38
flying fish 40–1

gills 12, 13, 14
goby 6
Great Barrier Reef 46

habitats 46

jawless fish 4, 5, 44

kangal fish (doctor fish) 43
krill 19, 27

lampreys 5, 44
lion-fish 36
lungfish 14–15

marlin 9

parasites 4, 42, 44
parrotfish 18, 39
pike 20, 21
piranha fish 22
plankton 26, 27
poison see venom
predators 7, 19, 30, 48
pufferfish 37

rays 5, 10, 34
remora fish 9, 42

salmon 30–1
scales 6
scavengers 18
seahorses 32–3, 47
sensors 6, 11, 34
sharks 4, 5, 7, 11, 18, 19,
    23, 24–7, 28, 29, 42
shoals 22
snakefish 20, 21
spawning 30, 31
speed 4, 9, 25
spotted handfish 48–9
stonefish 36, 39
sturgeon 4, 49
surgeonfish 36
swordfish 4, 9

tuna 4, 19, 48, 50, 51

venom (poison) 10, 36, 37

whales 19
wrasse 29, 42, 43

zebra-fish 37

Series in the *Freestyle Curriculum Strand* include:

Turbulent Planet

Energy Essentials

Incredible Creatures

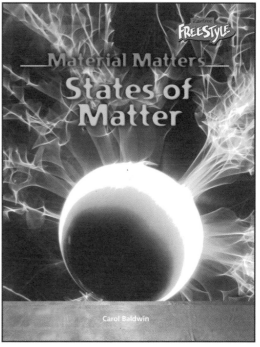

Material Matters

Find out about the other titles in these series on our website www.raintreepublishers.co.uk